WOULD YOU RATHER...?

Over 300 CRAZY QUESTIONS!

Wonderfully

WEIRD

Justin Heimberg & David Gomberg

Published by Seven Footer Press
247 West 30th St., 2nd Fl.
New York, NY 10001
First Printing, June 2013
10 9 8 7 6 5 4 3 2
Manufactured in Baltimore, Maryland, 06/13
© Copyright Justin Heimberg and David Gomberg, 2013
All Rights Reserved

Design by Thomas Schirtz

ISBN 978-1934734-92-6

www.sevenfooterpress.com

TABLE OF CONTENTS

WEIRD IS THE NEW NORMAL

Hey, don't knock "Weird." Weird is in. Weird is cool. These days, there's something wrong with you if you aren't at least a little bit weird. Of course, there's weird, and then there's *WEIRD*! The questions in this book are definitely *WEIRD*! In fact, they're so strange, if there were a way to double-capitalize "weird," we would have done it...I guess we could have bolded it, come to think of it. Or underlined it...Or used a larger font...Hmm... Anyway, it's best to let the questions themselves prove how **_WEIRD!?_** this book really is. And just to clarify: the "weird" umbrella does include all the gross, fantastical, and embarrassing *Would You Rather...?* questions you've learned to both love and hate. So don't hold back as you enjoy contemplating the strange and silly. It's time to let your inner weirdo out.

HOW TO USE THIS BOOK

1 Sit around with a bunch of friends.

2 Read a question from the book out loud and talk about it.

You won't believe some of the stuff you'll come up with as you think about which choice to make.

3 Everybody must choose! That's the whole point. It forces you to really think about the options.

4 Once everyone has chosen, move on to the next question.

It's that simple. We have provided a few things to think about for some questions, but don't stop there. Much of the fun comes from imagining the different ways your choice will affect your life. Don't hold back as you discuss the options. Be silly, gross, and funny. There are no wrong answers, although some people might consider the questions themselves to be very very "wrong."

CHAPTER ONE

WEIRD

Would you rather...

a hermit crab make its home in your ear

OR

in your mouth?

Would you rather...

wake up each morning by your parents dumping a vat of iced Gatorade on your head like they do to winning football coaches

OR

by your bed popping you into the air like toast from an overactive toaster?

YOU MUST CHOOSE!

Would you rather...

naturally give off a strong Wi-Fi signal

OR

be able to make the sounds of a drum set by smacking different parts of your body?

YOU MUST CHOOSE!

3

Would you rather...

live in a house made entirely of flannel

OR

bounce-house material?

Would you rather...

slowly over time begin to look more and more like Abraham Lincoln

OR

slowly become lighter and lighter until you weigh as little as a helium balloon?

YOU MUST CHOOSE!

Would you rather...

burp Ping-Pong balls

OR

hiccup jelly beans?

Would you rather...

sneeze fireflies

OR

yawn hummingbirds?

YOU MUST CHOOSE!

Would you rather...

change your first name to any color

OR

to any texture?
Things to consider: Yellow Johnson, Silky-smooth McGee,
Magenta Miller, Gritty Goldstein

Follow up: What name would you choose?

YOU MUST CHOOSE!

Would you rather your school have...

chocolate syrup water fountains **OR** disco lights and music in the cafeteria?

moving sidewalk hallways **OR** recliner chairs in class?

Pittsburgh Steeler gym teachers **OR** remote-controlled janitors?

YOU MUST CHOOSE!

Would you rather...

be able to mute your teachers

OR

your parents?

Would you rather...

vomit raspberry sherbet

OR

fart Peyton Manning statistics?

YOU MUST CHOOSE!

Would you rather...

have a nose that grew like Pinocchio's whenever you lied

OR

a butt that expanded whenever you lied?

Would you rather...

have windshield wipers on your nostrils

OR

vacuum nostrils?

YOU MUST CHOOSE!

Would you rather...

have caffeinated saliva

OR

sparkly boogers?
Things to consider: always being jittery, glitter-sneezes

YOU MUST CHOOSE!

TRIPLE THREATS!

Here are some new twists on old favorites:

Would you rather...

fight Mike Tyson

OR

talk like him

OR

get his face tattoo?

YOU MUST CHOOSE!

Would you rather...

work for Donald Trump

OR

marry him

OR

comb your hair like him?

Would you rather...

wrestle The Rock

OR

shave your head like him

OR

have to wear his wrestling outfit in
public every day?

YOU MUST CHOOSE!

Would you rather...

there was a five-minute earthquake in your bedroom every night **OR** a two-minute downpour of rain?

a twenty-second tornado **OR** a six-inch snowfall?

a minute-long gazelle stampede **OR** a thirty-second cameo appearance by Tyler Perry?

YOU MUST CHOOSE!

Would you rather...

have auto-tinting eyeballs

OR

auto-tuned laughter?

Would you rather...

only be able to sleep between 2pm and 4pm

OR

only be able to eat between 3:08pm and 3:12 pm?
Things to consider: crankiness, competitive eating career

YOU MUST CHOOSE!

Would you rather...

immediately take anything that's ever handed to you and throw it as far as you can

OR

furiously lick it all over?

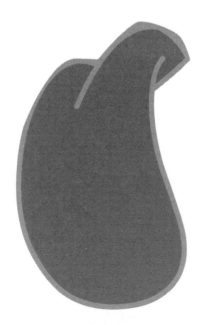

ACTION!

Whoever reads this must do one of the options below in front of everyone else in the room:

sing two verses of a patriotic song **OR** do a robot dance for 30 seconds

twenty seconds of air guitar **OR** forty seconds of air cello.

YOU MUST CHOOSE!

17

Better gym class unit?

Broadway dance **OR** pro wrestling?

Rock-Paper-Scissors **OR** mime?

planking **OR** cow-tipping?

Would you rather...

be raised by coyotes

OR

a pageant mother?

YOU MUST CHOOSE!

Would you rather...

be mortally terrified of ovals

OR

mulch?

Things to consider: Easter egg hunts in the yard, math class, mulch class

Would you rather...

have an echo with a snobby French accent

OR

a shadow that always has a sombrero and a huge handlebar mustache?

YOU MUST CHOOSE!

YOU CHOOSE!

Gandalf

OR

Dumbledore?

Fight a dragon with?

Roadtrip with?

As your soccer team's goalie?

As a friend on a double-date to a school dance?

YOU MUST CHOOSE!

CHAPTER TWO

POWERFUL POWERS OF POWER

Would you rather...

be able to eat excessively and give other people the weight gain

OR

add muscle just by watching others work out?

Would you rather...

have feet with retractable ice skating blades

OR

fingertips with paint brush hangnails?

YOU MUST CHOOSE!

Fart the Power.

Would you rather...

have heat farts **OR** freeze farts?

silenced farts **OR** megaphone farts?

electric guitar solo farts **OR** laser farts?

confetti farts **OR** farts that summon fish like Aquaman?

(This page paraphrased from the original Shakespeare.)

YOU MUST CHOOSE!

POWERFUL POWERS OF POWER

Would you rather...

have a "hype man" like rappers that hypes up your book reports at school

OR

a magical towel boy that appears during sports whenever you need to wipe sweat?

YOU MUST CHOOSE!

Are you the type to use your powers for good or evil?

Would you rather...

be able to cure headaches **OR** cause them?

be able to cure diarrhea **OR** cause it?

be able to cure the Harlem Shake **OR** cause it?

YOU MUST CHOOSE!

Would you rather...

have optional noise-cancelling headphones built into your ears

OR

binoculars built into your eyes?

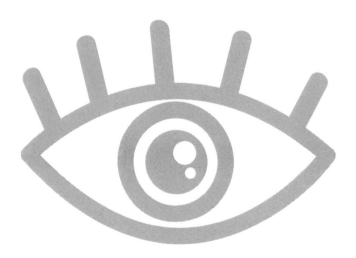

YOU MUST CHOOSE!

Would you rather...

inspire confidence in everyone you meet

OR

inspire high fives?
Things to consider: the first day of school, political career

Would you rather...

bite your tongue every fifth chew

OR

bite someone else's tongue?

YOU MUST CHOOSE!

Would you rather...

have to eat only once a month **OR** sleep only once a month?

have to shower only once a month **OR** pee only once a month?

have to brush your teeth only once a month **OR** draw a picture of an accountant balancing a salmon on his nose only once a month?

YOU MUST CHOOSE!

Would you rather...

have Iron Man's suit

OR

his money?

Would you rather...

move in slow motion when playing sports but in fast motion at all other times

OR

vice-versa?

YOU MUST CHOOSE!

YOU CHOOSE!

Avengers
OR
Justice League?

Fight crime with?

Fight against?

Play dodgeball with?

Play this book with?

YOU MUST CHOOSE!

POWERFUL POWERS OF POWER

33

Would you rather...

have a kangaroo pouch on the inside of your left thigh

OR

an inflatable air mattress built into your back?

YOU MUST CHOOSE!

Would you rather...

get straight A's for a year without working hard

OR

get straight B's for the rest of your life without working hard?

YOU MUST CHOOSE!

Would you rather...

be so rich you had personal bookmarkers who just stood around and kept their thumbs on the page you left off on

OR

have a convincing stunt double who could sit in on boring classes for you?

YOU MUST CHOOSE!

Would you rather...

receive a newsfeed that is one day in the future

OR

fifty years in the future?

Things to consider: lottery numbers, terrorist attacks, inventions, patience

Would you rather...

play this book with Jimmy Fallon

OR

your principal?

YOU MUST CHOOSE!

CHAPTER THREE

GROSS, GRODY, GRIMY, AND GRITTY[1]

---

[1]Also the names of rejected Smurfs

Would you rather...

only be able to eat spilled foods

OR

only be able to drink fluids that someone else has already gargled and spit out?

YOU MUST CHOOSE!

Would you rather...

have a "volcano zit" that spontaneously erupts

OR

leave a snail trail wherever you go?

YOU MUST CHOOSE!

43

WOULD YOU RATHER...ONLY AGE ON THE LEFT SIDE OF YOUR BODY

OR ON THE BOTTOM HALF?

Would you rather...

have caviar belly button lint

OR

sweat baked potato toppings?

Things to consider: working up a snack, constant laundry needs, opening up a restaurant

YOU MUST CHOOSE!

Which BLT would you rather eat?

Band-Aids (used), lice, and toe-cheese

OR

back-hair, larva, and tar?

Which BLT would you rather eat?

barf, lint, and tamales

OR

bass-scales, Listerine, and tortoise-eyes?

YOU MUST CHOOSE!

Would you rather...

clean all the chalkboards in your school with your tongue

OR

scrub the toilets with your bare hands?

YOU MUST CHOOSE!

Would you rather...

always have your underwear full of sand

OR

ketchup?

Would you rather...

swallow a tall glass of tadpoles

OR

eat a heaping bowl of caterpillars?

Things to consider: waiting a little while and then choosing between eating frogs or butterflies

YOU MUST CHOOSE!

Would you rather...have 30-inch-long earlobes

Or 8-inch-long eyelids?

49

Would you rather...

for $1,000, have to keep your mouth open as a spider webbed the entire opening

OR

have to lie still without moving for a minute as 500 centipedes crawl all over your body?

YOU MUST CHOOSE!

Would you rather live-Tweet...

as you get beat up by a bully **OR** as you run from an angry black bear?

your dentist appointment **OR** your bout with stomach flu?
Things to consider: 2 cavities :(; pukedx4#chunky

YOU MUST CHOOSE!

Would you rather...

have your eyeballs transferred to the end of your thumbs

OR

your nostrils moved to the end of your big toes?

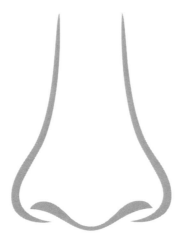

YOU MUST CHOOSE!

Would you rather...

have hair growing out of your ears **OR** out of your nostrils?

on your eyelids **OR** on your palms?

under your scalp **OR** on your irises?

YOU MUST CHOOSE!

Would you rather...

dip a chip in salsa made from squashed mosquitos

OR

from the liquid that collects at the bottom of your kitchen garbage can?

YOU MUST CHOOSE!

Boogers.

Would you rather have...

ruby boogers **OR** jade boogers?

interlocking boogers (like Legos) **OR** ladybug boogers?

SweeTart boogers **OR** candy corn boogers?

Follow up: Considering shape, taste, and size, what would your favorite candy booger be? Swedish Fish? Licorice? What else?

YOU MUST CHOOSE!

Would you rather...

save your place in this book using a live tapeworm

OR

a fleshy cow tongue?

YOU MUST CHOOSE!

Would you rather...

use wasabi toothpaste

OR

salami underpants?

Would you rather...

use nacho cheese shampoo

OR

maple syrup eye drops?

YOU MUST CHOOSE!

Would you rather...

have your mom pre-chew all your food

OR

only eat what you can find on the side of the road?

Would you rather...

kiss every animal in a petting zoo on the mouth once

OR

clean their cages five times?

YOU MUST CHOOSE!

Would you rather...

for a wedding ring, wear a tarantula whose legs are clutched around your finger

OR

use a greasy hair from an old weird guy that's tightly wrapped around your knuckle a few times?

YOU MUST CHOOSE!

CHAPTER FOUR

RICHES OF EMBARRASSMENT

Would you rather...

find out you accidentally blind-copied your entire
address book on every email over the past year

OR

that your diary has been WikiLeaked?

Would you rather...

fart while having an important meeting with the principal

OR

while talking to a girl/boy you have a crush on?

YOU MUST CHOOSE!

Would you rather...

have your first kiss live-streamed on the Internet

OR

the entirety of your first date recorded and analyzed on Sports Center?

Things to consider: slow-motion replay, statistics

YOU MUST CHOOSE!

Would you rather have only one dance...

"the confused robot" **OR** "the frightened duck?"

"the lost contact lens" **OR** "the bloated carpenter?"

"the plundering Viking" **OR** "the Whac-A-Mole?"

Action!
All of you have to choose to do one dance in each question above.

YOU MUST CHOOSE!

Would you rather...

have a group of rowdy hecklers follow you around to all your classes

OR

a panel of Olympic judges follow you around holding up scores for everything you do?

Things to consider: the Russian judge giving you a 3.6 on your coat-hanging

YOU MUST CHOOSE!

Would you rather...

have your dreams automatically uploaded to YouTube

OR

not?

Follow up: What about your daydreams?

What about your parents' daydreams?

YOU MUST CHOOSE!

Which epic fail would you rather go viral...

wiping out on your bike

OR

you snarfing milk?

YOU MUST CHOOSE!

ACTION!

Winner gets the best thing in the other's lunch.

Would you rather...

spell the title of this chapter correctly (don't look)

OR

challenge your friend to spell it?

YOU MUST CHOOSE!

Would you rather...

get a tattoo of your parents on your back

OR

have them get one of you on theirs?

Would you rather...

every time you trip and fall, have it published to Instagram

OR

every time you go to the bathroom, have Paul Revere ride through your city on his horse yelling "[YOUR NAME] is pooping! [YOUR NAME] is pooping!?

YOU MUST CHOOSE!

Would you rather...

when looking in a mirror, have your reflection always be naked

OR

wearing a veil?

Things to consider: public bathrooms, doing your hair

Would you... have your most embarrassing moment uploaded to YouTube to have your greatest accomplishments uploaded too?

YOU MUST CHOOSE!

Would you rather...

wear a pink tutu for a month

OR

the Sunday newspaper?

Would you rather...

only be able to walk Gangnam Style

OR

at 1/10 normal speed?

YOU MUST CHOOSE!

Would you rather...

have your life running with audible DVD-extra style commentary by insult comedians

OR

commentary by your parents?

YOU MUST CHOOSE!

Would you rather...

when typing, always replace "m" with "p"

OR

"f" for "d"?

Things to consider: darts, mommy, "mommy darts"

YOU MUST CHOOSE!

Would you rather...

have a big "ERROR!" message appear above your head whenever you are wrong

OR

a fat opera singer appear singing "THAAAATS-AH WROOOONG-OH!!!"?

YOU MUST CHOOSE!

C H A P T E R   F I V E

YOUR WILDEST DREAMS[1]

---

[1] Okay, maybe not your wildest

Would you rather...

your family own a self-driving car

OR

a self-stocking refrigerator?

YOU MUST CHOOSE!

WOULD YOU RATHER..."PHOTO-BOMB" THE PRESIDENTIAL FAMILY OFFICIAL PORTRAIT

OR GO BACK IN TIME AND "PAINTING-BOMB" THE MONA LISA?

Would you rather...

have a pack of ninjas sworn to protect you **OR** a pack of ostriches?

a pack of electric eels **OR** a pack of toddlers?

a flock of butterflies **OR** a pack of living tortillas?

YOU MUST CHOOSE!

Would you rather...

have your music teacher be Cee Lo Green

OR

your science teacher be the guys from *Mythbusters*?

Would you rather...

live on an Amish farm for a year

OR

with the Inuit for a year?

YOU MUST CHOOSE!

Would you rather...

have your face on the heads side of the United States nickel

OR

your butt on the tails side?

YOU MUST CHOOSE!

Would you rather...

have the power to read your parents' minds

OR

your friends' diaries?

Would you rather...

swap your mom with Michelle Obama for a week

OR

with Angelina Jolie?

YOU MUST CHOOSE!

Would you rather...

receive a bad Botox injection to your face resulting in a permanent expression of surprise

OR

disgust?

Action!

Make these expressions and hold them for as long as you can.

YOU MUST CHOOSE!

Would you rather...

have a backpack that magically did your homework

OR

chores that completed themselves?

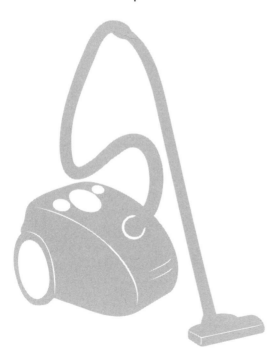

YOU MUST CHOOSE!

Would you rather...

have the country renamed after you

OR

be able to name the school anything you wanted to?

Follow Up: What would you name it?

YOU MUST CHOOSE!

Who would you rather have on your basketball team...

Spiderman **OR** Batman?

Green Lantern **OR** the Flash?

Iron Man **OR** the Hulk?

YOU MUST CHOOSE!

Would you rather...

have a tree that grows apples that look exactly like you

OR

a yard of flowers that pay you compliments when they see you?

Would you rather...

go to a school that's a giant fun house

OR

one big water park?

YOU MUST CHOOSE!

Would you rather...

be able to take each school lesson simply by swallowing a daily pill

OR

be able to get in good jogging shape just by watching cartoons?

Would you rather...

have spit that turns into blow darts

OR

hair that turns into tarantulas when cut?

YOU MUST CHOOSE!

Would you rather...

have a fortune teller tell you that you have five years to live, but it will be the best and most exciting years of your life

OR

you will live for 100 years, but it will be mostly boring?

YOU MUST CHOOSE!

Would you rather...

be declared head of your household and make all the rules at home

OR

be able to set all school rules?

Follow up: What rules would you make?

YOU MUST CHOOSE!

Would you rather...

be able to see for 1,000 miles

OR

hear for 500 miles?

Would you rather...

taste anything being eaten within twenty feet

OR

smell anything within fifty feet?

YOU MUST CHOOSE!

Would you rather...

be half-person/half-horse

OR

half-person/half-eagle?

Would you rather...

be half-person/half-kangaroo

OR

half-person/half-spider?

Would you rather...

be half-person/half-toilet

OR

half-person/half-dreidel?

YOU MUST CHOOSE!

Would you rather...

only be able to go to One Direction concerts for musical entertainment

OR

only be able to go literally one direction forever (you can never turn; you just keep going one way)?

Things to consider: career choice, raising a family, moving West each year

YOU MUST CHOOSE!

Would you rather...

have a network of secret tunnels leading to your friends' houses

OR

have a teleportation device from your home to two places of your choice?

Follow up: What two places would you choose?

YOU MUST CHOOSE!

Would you rather be a Transformer who changes into...

a helicopter **OR** a tank?

a blender **OR** an electric guitar?

a muffin tray **OR** crutches?

YOU MUST CHOOSE!

CHAPTER SIX

REALLY WEIRD

Would you rather...

have your nose rotate on your face based on the time of day like the hands of a clock

OR

have your eyeballs rise and set with the sun?

Things to consider: things looking up in the morning, noon

YOU MUST CHOOSE!

Zombie or werewolf? You decide!

Become one?

As a roommate?

As a dentist?

Vampire or Mummy? You decide!

Share bunk beds with?

Play a game of one-on-one basketball against?

Pack your lunch?

YOU MUST CHOOSE!

WOULD YOU RATHER...HAVE TO SLEEP EACH NIGHT ON AN AIRPORT LUGGAGE CONVEYOR BELT

OR ON A SKI LIFT?

Would you rather...

talk like Bane from *Batman* whenever ordering food

OR

have occasional Whac-a-Mole's pop out from your nostrils and ears that need to be poked back in?

YOU MUST CHOOSE!

Would you rather catch a strange virus where you temporarily vomit...

sprinkles **OR** Gummy Bears?

quarters **OR** lottery tickets?

hot fudge **OR** helium?

Things to consider: What would the last one sound like?

YOU MUST CHOOSE!

REALLY WEIRD

Would you rather...

have poison ivy (the rash) on your palms

OR

have poison ivy (the plant) on your palms?

Things to consider: shaking hands

YOU MUST CHOOSE!

Would you rather...

be continuously stalked by a cowboy who is always trying to creep up on you and slap drinks out of your hand

OR

by a ninja who sneaks up on you and tickles you before running off giggling?

YOU MUST CHOOSE!

Would you rather...

have a telepathic remote control connection to the TV

OR

have your favorite memories saved on your DVR?

Would you rather...

be caught in an avalanche of marshmallows

OR

in a whirlpool of banana milkshake?

YOU MUST CHOOSE!

Would you rather...

have all of your family arguments decided by jury

OR

by dance-off?

Things to consider: your mom, your dad, your siblings, your grandparents

YOU MUST CHOOSE!

Would you rather...

have an iPad built into your stomach

OR

be able to dispense various types of soda through your fingertips?

Would you rather...

be able to deep-fry things by staring at them intensely

OR

be able to drink things by singing to them?

YOU MUST CHOOSE!

Would you rather...

be unable to see anything purple

OR

be unable to read any word with a "y" in it?

Things to consider: Do xzq know what this kxzq?

YOU MUST CHOOSE!

Would you rather have the ability to control things that rhyme with...

"dog" **OR** "cat"?

"bite" **OR** "blip"?

"orange" **OR** "arugula"?

Things to consider: What sort of things would you control?

YOU MUST CHOOSE!

Would you rather...

salivate hot chocolate (with full size marshmallows)

OR

Cherry Coke (with crushed ice)?

Would you rather...

be able to only drink tomato juice the rest of your life

OR

have to bathe in it?

YOU MUST CHOOSE!

Would you rather...

have every fifth room you walk into suddenly turn into a karaoke bar

OR

a yoga studio?

Would you rather...

sleep in a giant manila envelope

OR

packaged in bubble wrap?

YOU MUST CHOOSE!

Would you rather...

have your only eating tool be a pair of tweezers

OR

a single chopstick?

Would you rather...

possess a toaster

OR

be possessed by one?

YOU MUST CHOOSE!

CHAPTER SEVEN

COOL AND UNUSUAL PUNISHMENTS

Would you rather...

put on a pair of duct tape underwear

OR

use a cactus pillow?

Things to consider: you have to eventually take the pants off (or do you?); dimples

YOU MUST CHOOSE!

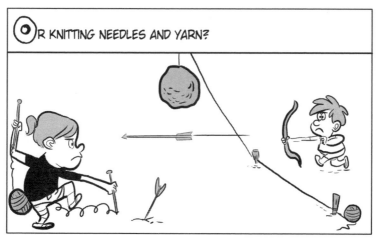

Would you rather...

have webbed hands and feet

OR

a duckbill?

Would you rather...

be pelted with 100 raw eggs

OR

have to swallow 10 of them?

YOU MUST CHOOSE!

Would you rather battle in the wild...

100 frogs **OR** 1,000 butterflies?

a cross-eyed lion **OR** a gassy cheetah?

a 6-foot Swedish meatball **OR** a 6-foot cube of lime Jell-O (with fruit in it)?

YOU MUST CHOOSE!

Would you rather...

only work out your left arm until it has way more muscle than the rest of your body

OR

only work out your right leg?

YOU MUST CHOOSE!

Would you rather...

have an uncuttable 7-inch long hangnail on your thumb

OR

a one-inch long eyelash permanently stuck in your eye?

Would you rather...

always have sunburn

OR

always have a painless suntan, but have it be striped?

YOU MUST CHOOSE!

WOULD YOU RATHER...HAVE ANTLERS ON YOUR HEAD

OR ON YOUR BUTT?

Would you rather...

use fish-flavored Chapstick

OR

wet dog-scented deodorant?

Would you rather...

have everyone in the world be extremely allergic to you

OR

vice-versa?

YOU MUST CHOOSE!

Would you rather...

mop up the area under your refrigerator with your tongue

OR

eat a cotton candy made from vacuum cleaner contents?

Would you rather...

take a shot in the gut point blank from a T-shirt cannon

OR

be shot from the T-shirt cannon?

YOU MUST CHOOSE!

Would you rather...

walk barefoot on a beach with sand made of fire ants

OR

thumbtacks?

Would you rather...

play ultimate Frisbee with a bee-covered honeycomb

OR

basketball with an iron-hot ball?

Things to consider: never getting open

YOU MUST CHOOSE!

You just received a wasp nest for your birthday.

Would you rather...

wear it as a turban

OR

use it as a piñata?

Would you rather...

use it as a pillow

OR

as a boot?

YOU MUST CHOOSE!

Would you rather...

receive an electric shock every time you blink **OR** with every step you take?

every time you sneeze **OR** every time you fall asleep?

every time you exhale **OR** whenever seated?

YOU MUST CHOOSE!

Would you rather...

as a gladiator, battle 1,000 grasshoppers

OR

20 sock puppets?

Would you rather...

have the joints in your body replaced with rusty hinges

OR

your skin covered with papier-mâché?

Things to consider: being mistaken for a piñata, oiling when stiff

YOU MUST CHOOSE!

Would you rather...

have a magnetic forehead

OR

a suction cup-covered butt?

Things to consider: taking a bath

YOU MUST CHOOSE!

Would you rather...

reach into a cookie jar filled with angry crayfish

OR

with an overly affectionate octopus?

YOU MUST CHOOSE!

Would you rather...

ride on a carousel where all the horses have been replaced by porcupines

OR

by blocks of dry ice?

Would you rather...

be stuck for a week on a life raft with a boa constrictor

OR

a leopard?

Things to consider: How would you survive?

YOU MUST CHOOSE!

CHAPTER EIGHT

POP GOES THE CULTURE!

SPORTS
Would you rather...

be an NFL lineman **OR** a punter?

receiver **OR** running back?

referee **OR** mascot?

YOU MUST CHOOSE!

What would you add to the Olympic games if you were in charge?

Competitive Eating **OR** Food-fighting?

Planking **OR** Slap Fights?

Rock-Paper-Scissors **OR** Competitive Coughing?

YOU MUST CHOOSE!

Would you rather...

be a professional soccer player

OR

a professional quidditch player?

YOU MUST CHOOSE!

Would you rather...

watch a football game played by ballerinas

OR

a ballet performed by football players?

Would you rather...

see a sport that was a combination of football and rock-climbing

OR

hockey and ice-fishing?

Things to consider: choosing a direction after winning the coin toss

YOU MUST CHOOSE!

Would you rather...

have Lionel Messi on your kickball team

OR

RG3 on your dodgeball team?

Would you rather...

find a fly in your soup

OR

a soup in your fly?

YOU MUST CHOOSE!

Would you rather...

play Capture the Flag with a horde of zombies

OR

rugby with a pack of werewolves?

YOU MUST CHOOSE!

TECHNOLOGY
Would you rather...

have to text with your tongue

OR

have your text messages edited by your mom?

YOU MUST CHOOSE!

Would you rather...

have everything you design in Minecraft come to life

OR

live out a real version of the video game Halo?

Better invention...?

pants that charge your phone by the static electricity generated while you walk

OR

"cheezers" (little tweezers you use to eat Cheetos and Doritos to keep your fingers clean)?

YOU MUST CHOOSE!

Which would you rather use as a cellphone case...

a beehive **OR** a kiln?

a burrito **OR** your friend's back pocket?

a dead flounder **OR** a working toaster?

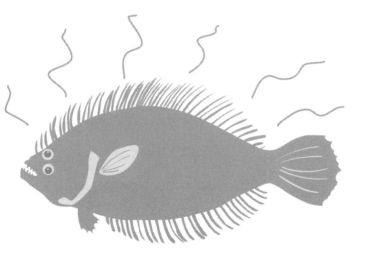

YOU MUST CHOOSE!

Would you rather...

have the ability to create a Wi-Fi hotspot for as long as you continue to tap-dance

OR

be able to communicate telepathically but only in Vietnamese?

YOU MUST CHOOSE!

Would you rather...

have a Nintendo DS that can only be played at ten times normal volume

OR

with a one-inch screen?

Would you rather...

be able to receive Tweets only about photosynthesis

OR

only be able to send Tweets containing facts about Bolivia?

YOU MUST CHOOSE!

FASHION
Would you rather...

have eyebrows shaped like M's **OR** W's?

V's **OR** S's on their sides?

@ symbols **OR** &'s?

YOU MUST CHOOSE!

Would you rather...

dress from the 1700s

OR

the 2700s?

Things to consider: three-cornered hats of the past; nine-cornered hats of the future

YOU MUST CHOOSE!

Would you rather...

have earrings that were paper-weights **OR** kites?

working light bulbs **OR** Ping Pong paddles?

fruit bats **OR** the keys to the bathrooms at the local Exxon station?

Would you rather...

wear an Eskimo coat all summer

OR

a tiny bathing suit all winter?

YOU MUST CHOOSE!

Would you rather...

to an important event, wear a lettuce toupee

OR

a cauliflower corsage?

YOU MUST CHOOSE!

Would you rather...

always wear a hoodie with the drawstring completely pulled

OR

a belt latched five notches too tight?

Things to consider: field of vision

YOU MUST CHOOSE!

Would you rather...

have to always be posing like a fashion model during a shoot

OR

have to always walk like a runway model?

Things to consider: taking notes in class, walking to school

YOU MUST CHOOSE!

Would you rather...

have to always have only one shoe on

OR

three shoes on (with one on your hand)?

Would you rather...

wear a post-it note tuxedo/wedding dress to your wedding

OR

a bacon cummerbund/veil?

YOU MUST CHOOSE!

Would you rather...

be required to wear a top hat to school **OR** a cape?

shoes twenty sizes too large **OR** ½ shirts (having one arm hole and covering only one side of your body)?

shirts made of Saran Wrap **OR** pants made of tin foil?

clothes made entirely of rubber bands **OR** streamers?

YOU MUST CHOOSE!

ENTERTAINMENT

Would you rather...

watch only your favorite TV show

OR

be able to watch everything else but not your favorite?

Would you rather...

live in the world of Angry Birds

OR

Temple Run?

YOU MUST CHOOSE!

Would you rather...

have the voice of a whiny Optimus Prime

OR

a sarcastic Scooby Doo?

YOU MUST CHOOSE!

Would you rather battle in the Hunger Games armed with:

a slingshot **OR** a club?

a bowling ball **OR** a hockey stick and puck?

salad bar ingredients **OR** a baguette, a pimento, and a picture of Ponce de León?

YOU MUST CHOOSE!

Would you rather...

your parents were zombies **OR** vampires?

witches **OR** werewolves?

giant mice **OR** Justin Bieber clones?

YOU MUST CHOOSE!

Would you rather...

get angry like the Incredible Hulk

OR

be a Reverse Hulk (turn into a huge green monster like the Hulk when you are calm and become normal only when very angry?)

Things to consider: potential for damage, trying to be angry

YOU MUST CHOOSE!

Would you rather...

have Pokémons created based on the people in your school

OR

a Broadway musical?

YOU MUST CHOOSE!

Would you rather...

have Tosh.0 do a monologue making fun of you

OR

have every new song that Taylor Swift writes be about you and the bad things you did?

Would you rather...

be hunted by minotaurs

OR

real-life Minecraft creepers?

YOU MUST CHOOSE!

Would you rather...

for the rest of your life, only be able to purchase things out of the Skymall catalog

OR

from Snoop Lion's garage sales?

YOU MUST CHOOSE!

CHAPTER NINE

PHILOSOPHICAL NONSENSE

Would you rather...

begin to age backward at age 25

OR

not?

30?

35?

40?

45?

50?

YOU MUST CHOOSE!

Would you rather...

live in a world populated exclusively by clones of you

OR

not?

Would you rather...

in a zombie war, join the horde

OR

run from it?

YOU MUST CHOOSE!

Would you rather...

have the perfect girlfriend/boyfriend but only you can see and hear them

OR

have a girlfriend/boyfriend that everyone thinks is great but is a jerk in private?

YOU MUST CHOOSE!

Would you rather...

have the skull shape of a cave man

OR

his posture?

Would you rather...

be able to travel through time in a magic bumper car

OR

travel through space on a magic tricycle?

Know Your Limit

Would you rather...

have the number of times you can walk through a door-way per day be limited to 5 **OR** the number of times you can stand up (from being seated or lying down) limited to 5 per day?

30 chews per day **OR** 100 steps per day?

3 questions per day **OR** 3 bad words per day?

YOU MUST CHOOSE!

Would you rather...

have the knowledge that there is a missile launcher somewhere in the world that is always aimed directly at you

OR

that one of the meals that you are served in the next ten years will be poisoned?

YOU MUST CHOOSE!

Would you rather...

only speak using words with one syllable

OR

rhyme all the time?

Things to consider: It might be bad to have one curse, but to have both it would be worse. If this is how you must now speak, you may be sick in just a week.

YOU MUST CHOOSE!

Would you rather...

have to drive ¼ the speed limit

OR

4 times the speed limit?

Would you rather...

experience life three seconds in the future

OR

three seconds in the past?

YOU MUST CHOOSE!

Fun with homonyms

Would you rather...

always see in night vision

OR

knight vision (through a knight's helmet)?

Would you rather...

always have morning breath

OR

mourning breath (your breath causes people to start crying when you stand close to them)?

YOU MUST CHOOSE!

Would you rather...

believe in everything

OR

nothing?

YOU MUST CHOOSE!

Would you rather be reincarnated as...

a butterfly **OR** a mole?

a nerdy polar bear **OR** a popular penguin?

a parallelogram **OR** the number 694?

YOU MUST CHOOSE!

Would you rather...

look like this

OR

like this?

YOU MUST CHOOSE!

Would you rather...

be unable to tell the difference between chandeliers and mistletoe

OR

tissues and lettuce?

Things to consider: making a salad, blowing your nose, topping your hamburger, crying

YOU MUST CHOOSE!

Would you rather...

be the Greek god of lids

OR

the Greek god of dimmers?
Follow up: How would you use your powers?

Would you rather...

be bullied online

OR

offline?

YOU MUST CHOOSE!

Would you rather...

be stuck forever in autumn **OR** spring?

winter **OR** summer?

a wind tunnel **OR** a pool of nougat?

YOU MUST CHOOSE!

Would you rather...

be able to magically teleport to any place you've ever visited

OR

require no sleep to live?

Would you rather...

be able to meet friends in collective dreams at night

OR

be able to communicate telepathically but with a stutter?

YOU MUST CHOOSE!

Vocabulous!

Who says *Would You Rather...?* isn't educational?
Decide on the questions below and then look up the
words. Or vice-versa.

Would you rather...

be ambidextrous **OR** amphibious?

soporific **OR** misanthropic?

beneficent **OR** malevolent?

YOU MUST CHOOSE!

Would you rather...

quadruple your allowance but only be able to buy things from the 99 cent store

OR

double your allowance but only be able to buy things at the 99 dollar store?

Would you rather...

have the ability to pause your aging process twice in your life for five years each time

OR

have the ability to adjust your height?

YOU MUST CHOOSE!

Would you rather...

only be able to read in Spanish **OR** speak in French?

think in German **OR** dream in Russian?

get angry in Yiddish **OR** fart in Japanese?

YOU MUST CHOOSE!

Would you rather...

reverse sadness and happiness when reacting to things

OR

reverse anger and gratitude?

Would you rather...

have the power to predict Pat Sajak's future

OR

read Dikembe Mutombo's mind?

YOU MUST CHOOSE!

CHAPTER TEN

WOULD YOU...

Would you... limit your wardrobe to neon yellow clothes to be guaranteed to live to age 100?

Would you... never talk to your best friend again to be able to become friends with any celebrity of your choosing?

Would you... accept the ability to fly if you could only do it naked?
Things to consider: What would your super hero name be?

Would you... paint like the great artists of the Renaissance if you had to dress like them too?

YOU MUST CHOOSE!

Would you... permanently shrink by one foot to be able to dunk?

Would you... take one swat by a grizzly bear to get your own reality show?

Would you... get "Bieber Rulz" tattooed across your forehead for an unlimited supply of doughnut holes?
Your thigh?
The bottom of your foot?

Would you... do a monthly, naked shoulder-roll through poison ivy to maintain your internet access?

YOU MUST CHOOSE!

Would you... spend a week in January in an igloo built in your front yard to spend the whole summer at the beach?

Would you take this deal?

Every time you lie down, a massage therapist comes and gives you a ten minute relaxation massage, but every time you sit down in a reclined position, a dentist appears and starts to work on your teeth.

Would you... permanently change your bedtime to 8pm to have a Cartoon Network show made about you?

Would you... wear a superhero outfit every day in order to have a popular comic book based on your life?

YOU MUST CHOOSE!

Would you... change your name to Farterio Flatulencé for a free Ferrari?

Would you... eat a Quiznos sandwich every meal for a year in order to have them name a sandwich after you?

Would you... dye yourself purple to automatically ace every test at school?
Follow up: How long would you stay purple?

YOU MUST CHOOSE!

CHAPTER TWELVE

12

REALLY, REALLY WEIRD

Would you rather...

only be able to sleep in funeral caskets

OR

baby cribs?

Things to consider: slumber parties

Would you rather...

only be able to eat cold foods

OR

drink hot drinks?

YOU MUST CHOOSE!

Would you rather...

cry like a baby every time you see toast

OR

have a stealthy face painter paint your face like a kitten every time you fall asleep?

Would you rather...

go to a school that was totally punk rock

OR

totally steampunk?

YOU MUST CHOOSE!

What snot to love?

hot sauce **OR** glue?

stain remover **OR** applesauce?

Dippin' Dots **OR** Spiderman webbing?

YOU MUST CHOOSE!

Would you rather...

have your sibling replaced by a pot-bellied pig

OR

your parents replaced by two gruff old blues musicians?

YOU MUST CHOOSE!

Would you rather...

have to drink everything from a series of thimbles

OR

a glass that has never been washed?

Things to consider: drinking after a basketball game; what others will think of you

Would you rather...

only be able to talk if someone pulls a string on your back

OR

only be able to go the bathroom if someone walks you there with a leash?

YOU MUST CHOOSE!

Would you rather...

be vain

OR

veiny?

Would you rather...

live in a world where we communicated by a language of blinking

OR

slapping?

YOU MUST CHOOSE!

Would you rather...

have a Silly Putty tongue

OR

jetpack nostrils?

Would you rather...

your history teacher be Joe Biden

OR

your art teachers be Blue Man Group?

YOU MUST CHOOSE!

Would you rather...

have clockwork insides that need to be wound daily like a watch

OR

be the middle child in a family of Russian nesting dolls?

Would you rather...

see pixilated

OR

be pixilated?

YOU MUST CHOOSE!

Would you rather...

say the last word of your sentence in an over-exaggerated French accent

OR

as if asking a question?

Would you rather...

be able to speak fluent Chinese, but suffer from terrible loud gas every time you do

OR

speak fluent Russian but become increasingly exhausted as you do?

YOU MUST CHOOSE!

Would you rather...

sneeze lava

OR

belch laughing gas?

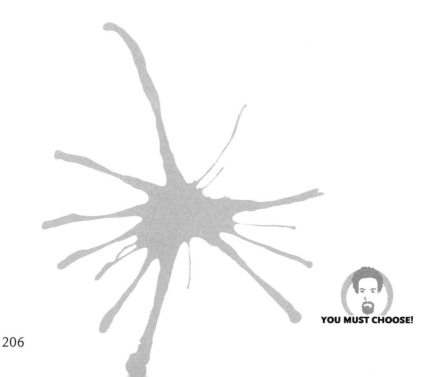

YOU MUST CHOOSE!

Would you rather...

have to make all your points through knock-knock jokes

OR

ghost stories?

Things to consider:
Knock, knock.
Who's there?
Dumb.
Dumb who?
Dumb question, that's what that is.

And when the girl turned around, standing right there was the ghost with a hook for a hand! (on which was a piece of paper that said, "What a dumb question!")

YOU MUST CHOOSE!

Would you rather...

whenever listening to music on your phone, have to play it at full volume

OR

have to share the other ear bud with a mysterious drifter named Sal?

Would you rather...

when you sleep, snore banjo music

OR

dream only of highlights of old 1970s ABA power forwards?

YOU MUST CHOOSE!

Would you rather...

always feel like you're walking on ice

OR

always feel like a 40 mile-per-hour wind is blowing in your face?

Would you rather...

only eat food that is "fun-sized"

OR

super-sized?

YOU MUST CHOOSE!

Would you rather...

live the rest of your life with binoculars glued to your eyes so that everything looks super close-up

OR

binoculars glued backwards to your head so everything looks super far away?

Would you rather...

always face North like a compass

OR

always move around as if playing basketball defense?

YOU MUST CHOOSE!

Would you rather...

automatically cheek-kiss everyone you meet for the first time

OR

automatically slap them?

Would you rather...

have one hand that weighs forty pounds

OR

one foot that is as light as a helium balloon?

YOU MUST CHOOSE!

Would you rather...

have a motion-activated smile

OR

flap about at all times like one of those inflatable tube men?

Would you rather...

have night lights built into your big toes

OR

Bluetooth earphones built into them?

YOU MUST CHOOSE!

Would you rather...

only remember things that happened on Tuesdays

OR

during the month of June?

Would you rather...

have a possessed credit card

OR

a possessed autocorrect?

YOU MUST CHOOSE!

Would you rather...

have hairy knuckles

OR

mossy toes?

Things to consider: Which is the better band name?

Would you rather...

have the ability to carbonate any liquid

OR

be able to see your future by staring into toilets?

YOU MUST CHOOSE!

Would you rather...

wear a scarf made of spider-filled cobwebs

OR

a tie of braided live snakes?

Would you rather...

inhale a gnat with every breath

OR

exhale silver spray paint with every breath?

YOU MUST CHOOSE!

Check out
wouldyourather.com
for more
questions and fun!

YOU WON'T BELIEVE YOUR EYES!

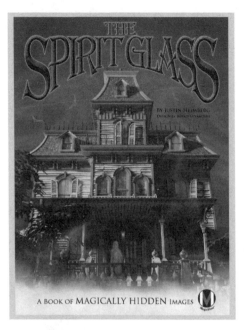

As you slide the Spirit Glass across the page, strange things begin to happen... Ghosts emerge from the mist, images take shape in crystal balls, secret messages magically appear. For each of twelve imaginative spreads, you must use the Spirit Glass to confront the challenge before you: Find ten ghosts in a haunted house. Search for nine skeletons hidden by the graveyard sky. Uncover hidden messages in invisible spider webs. If you do, you just might unlock the power of... The Spirit Glass!

 TheSpiritGlass.com

Go online to TheSpiritGlass.com and use the book to solve a supernatural mystery full of riddles, challenges, and puzzles. Winners will be eligible to be used as a ghost in a future book.

Seven Footer Kids

SEE THE UNSEEN!

Become a ghost hunter with MagicView™, an amazing, new, interactive reading experience unlike anything you've ever seen (or haven't seen!) before. Now you can live out the adventure, joining the characters as they reveal fingerprints, peer into crystal balls, or stare down the ever-changing face of a menacing apparition. Each hidden image is another clue in an awesome supernatural mystery that will amaze readers of any age.

MagicView™

GhostsofRockville.com